Mel Bay Presents

CHILDREN SING
Around the World.

Favorite Children's Songs from Many Lands!

By Jerry Silverman

Contents

Vrt' Sa, Děvča
Whirl Around Me

Czechoslovakia

Vrt' sa děv – ča, vrt' sa děv – ča o – ko – lo mňa.
Whirl a – round me, whirl a – round me, my pret – ty girl.

Vrt' sa děv – ča vrt' sa děv – ča o – ko – lo mňa.
Whirl a – round me, whirl a – round me, my pret – ty girl.

U – dě – laj ko – leč – ko, mo – ja ga – la – neč – ko,
Cir – cle – all a – bout – me, you can't do with – out me,

Bu – deš mo – ja, bu – deš mo – ja.
You will be mine, you will be mine

3

Vigndig A Fremd Kind
Rocking Someone Else's Child

(The Baby Sitter's Complaint)

Jewish (from Poland)

Zolst a – zoy le – bn Un zayn ge – zint, Vi ich __ vel dir zi – tsn Un
You can im – ag – ine, It drives me wild, To sit __ here all day And to

Chorus

vi – gn s'kind. Ay – lyu – lyu, Sha – sha – sha! Dayn
rock this child. Hush – a – bye, Don't you cry! Your

ma – me – shi z'ge – gan – gen in mark a – rayn. Ay – lyu – lyu,
ma – ma she has gone out, some food to buy. Hush a – bye,

Shlof, mayn kind, Di ma – me – shi vet ku – men gich un gshvind.
Sleep, my child; your ma – ma will re – turn in just a while.

4

Zolst azoy lebn,
S'geyt mir derinen!
Dayn mameshi z'gegangen
In mark arayn fardinen. *Chorus*

Andere meydelech
Tantsen un shpringen,
Un ich muzn' kind
Vign un zingen! *Chorus*

Andere meydelech
Tsukerkelech nashn,
Un ich muzn's kind
Vindelech vashn! *Chorus*

I can't take it,
It's just not fair —
Your mother has gone off
To work somewhere. *Chorus*

Other young girls
Dance and play,
While here by the cradle
I must stay. *Chorus*

Other young girls
Candies are *noshing**
And I've got a pile of
Diapers for washing. *Chorus*

*noshing-snacking, nibbling

5

Hazasodik A Tücsök
The Cricket's Wedding

Hungary

Háza-so-dik a tü-csök, szú-nyog lá-nyat ké-ri,
Mis-ter crick-et takes a wife, the mos-qui-to's daugh-ter.

Csi-szeg cso-szog a te-tü, nász nagy a-kar len-ni,
Shuf-fling comes the best-man louse, he's the groom's sup-port-er.

O-da-ug-rik a bó-ha, vő-fény a-kar len-ni,
Hop-ping comes the brides-maid flea, she is so ex-cit-ed,

Min-den-fé-le csúf bo-gár ven-dég a-kar len-ni
An-i-mals both great and small, all have been in-vit-ed.

Gólya volt a szekundás, kis béka a flótás
Dongódarázs a brúgos, pulyka volt a primás.
Táncba ugrik a majom, megjárja a polkát,
Híres betyár a bagoly, lesi hurkáját.

Farkas volt a mészáros, hat ökröt levágott,
A mellé még malacot ötvenet megfojtott.
Kecske volt a szakácsne, jó gulyáshúst főzött note:
Mig az ebéd elkészült, a tucsok megszökött!

Second fiddle is the stork, flutist frog is perky,
Hornets play the double-bass, fiddle one is turkey,
Merrily the monkey jumps, finds the polka pleasing,
While the rougueish old screech-owl bagpipe is a-squeezing.

Butcher-wolf six oxen felled for the wedding banquet,
And not satisfied with that, added fifty piglets.
Then the goat, a goulash served — all their buttons popped off,
But before they turned around, the sly cricket hopped off.

Langt Udi Skoven
Deep In the Forest

Denmark

1. Langt u – di sko – ven laa et lit – le bjerg, Al – drig saa jeg saa
   Deep in the for – est stands a lit – tle hill, I nev – er saw so

dej – ligt et bjerg, Bjer –get lig – ger langt____ ud – i sko – ven.
sweet a lit – tle hill, And the hill stands deep ____ in the for – est.

2. Paa det lil – le bjerg der stod et lil – le træ; Al – drig saa jey saa dej – ligt et træ;
   On the lit – tle hill there grew a lit – tle tree, I ne – ver saw so sweet a lit – tle tree;

Repeat cumulatively back to "tree" as song progresses.

Træ – et paa bjer – get, Bjer– get lig – ger langt____ ud – i sko – ven.
Tree on the hill,___ And the hill stands deep____ in the for – est.

3 Paa det lille træ var en lille gren,

4 Paa det lille gren der var en lille kvist,

5 Paa den lille kvist der var et lille blad,

6 Paa det lille blad der var en lille rede,

7 I den lille rede var et lille æg,

8 Af det lille æg der kom en lille fugl,

9 Paa den lille fugl der sad en lille fjer,

10 Af den lille fjer der blev en lille pude,

11 Paa den lille pude laa en lille dreng,
    Aldrig saa jeg saa dejlig en dreng,
    Drengen paa puden,
    Puden af jeren,
    Fjeren paa fuglen,
    Fuglen af ægget,
    Ægget i reden,
    Reden paa bladet,
    Bladen paa kvisten,
    Kvisten paa træet,
    Grenen paa træet,
    Træet paa bjerget,
    Bjerget ligger langt udi skoven.

3 On the little tree there grew a little branch,

4 On the little branch there grew a little twig,

5 On the little twig there grew a little leaf,

6 On the little leaf there was a little nest,

7 In the little nest there lay a little egg,

8 From the little egg there came a little bird,

9 On the little bird there grew a little feather,

10 From the little feather came a little pillow,

11 On the little pillow lay a little boy
    I never saw so sweet a little boy,
    Boy on the pillow,
    Pillow from the feather,
    Feather on the bird,
    Bird from the egg,
    Egg in the nest,
    Nest on the leaf,
    Leaf on the twig,
    Twig on the branch,
    Branch on the tree,
    Tree on the hill,
    And the hill stands deep in the forest.

Het Singelshuis
The Splendid House

Belgium (Flemish)

In Hol – land staat een huis, In Hol – land staat een
In Hol – land stands a house, In Hol – land stands a

huis, In Hol – land staat een sin – gels – huis. Hop – sa – sa,
house, In Hol – land stands a splen – did – house Hop – sa – sa,

sin – ge – lin – ge – la, In Hol – land staat een huis.
sin – ge – lin – ge – la, In Hol – land stands a house

Wie woont er in dat huis?	O, who lives in that house?
Wie woont er in dat huis?	O, who lives in that house?
Wie woont er in dat singelshuis?	O, who lives in that splendid house
Hopsasa, singelingela,	Hopsasa, singelingela,
Wie woont er in dat huis?	O, who lives in that house?

Daar woont al eenen boer.	It is a farmer's house.
Sa, boer waar is uw meid?	O farmer, where's your maid?
Mjin meid is in den stal.	My maid is in the barn.
Wat doet zij in den stal?	Why is she in the barn?
Daar mellekt zij de koe.	All for to milk the cow.
Wat doet zij met die melk?	What happens to the milk?
Daar kookt zij van een pap.	She makes a bowl of gruel.
Wat doet zij met die pap?	What happens to the gruel?
Die geeft zij aan haar kind.	She gives it to the child.
Wat doet zij met dat kind?	What happens to the child?
Dat zendt zij naar de school.	She sends it to the school.
Wat leert dat in de school?	What does it learn a school?
Daar leert het A-B-C.	It learns its A B C.

Cucul
Tsutsul

Yugoslavia (Macedonia)

Cu – cul pa – si___ go – ve – da, le – le, Cu – cul
Tsu – tsul grazed his___ herd of cows, le – le, Tsu – tsul

pa – si___ go – ve – da, Po – kraj re – ka
grazed his___ herd of cows, By the ri – ver

Sit – ni – ca, Po – kraj re – ka Sit – ni – ca.
Sit – ni – ca, By the ri – ver Sit – ni – ca.

Pominala lisica, le-le,
Pominala lisica.
Dobro utro, Cucule. (2)

Dal bog dobro, Lisico, le-le,
Dal bog dobro, Lisico,
Sto e vreva vo selo? (2)

Komarec se ženeše, le-le,
Komarec se ženeše,
Za mušička devojka. (2)

Petel drva cepeše, le-le,
Petel drva cepeše,
Kokoška 'i redeše. (2)

Mečka testo meseše, le-le,
Mečka testo meseše,
Mečeto go lapaše. (2)

Mister Fox, he did come by, le-le,
Mister Fox, he did come by.
Said, "Good morning, Tsutsule." (2)

"Hello, Fox," Tsutsul did say, le-le,
"Hello, Fox," Tsutsul did say,
"Tell me what's the news today." (2)

"Now the gnat won't be denied, le-le,
Now the gnat won't be denied,
For the fly will be his bride." (2)

"And the rooster's cutting wood, le-le,
And the rooster's cutting wood,
And the hen will stack it good." (2)

"Mama bear is kneading dough, le-le,
Mama bear is kneading dough,
For her cub, who loves it so." (2)

Oleana

Norway
By Ditmar Meidell

I O – le – a – na der er det godt at ____ væ _ re, i
In O – le – an – na, that is the place where I woud stay, In –

Nor – ge vil jeg in – te Sla – ve – læn – ken ____ bæ – re.
stead of bear – ing sla – v'ry's chains and suf – fer – ing in Nor – way.

Chorus
O – le O – le – a – na, O – le O – le – a ____ na,

O – le O – le O – le O – le O – le O – le – a _ na

I Oleana der faar
Jeg Jord for Intet,
Af Jorden voxer Kornet,
Og det gaar gesvindet det. *Chorus*

In Oleana, land they'll give you,
And it won't cost you a thing.
Grain, it will grow by itself,
While you just sit around and sing. *Chorus*

Aa Kornet det tærsker sig
Selv oppaa Laaven,
Imens ligger jeg aa
Hviler mig i Koven. *Chorus*

And then the grain will thresh itself
After the harvest,
While all I do is lie around.
That's the part that I like best. *Chorus*

Hej Markedsgang!
Poteterne skulde Du se, Du.
Der brændes mindst en Pot
Af hvereneste en Du. *Chorus*

At the market are for sale
The biggest spuds you e'er did see.
Each one yields a quart of whisky
At the distillery. *Chorus*

Ja Bayerøl saa godt,
Som han Ytteborg kan brygge,
Det risler i Bækkene
Til Fattigmandens Hygge. *Chorus*

Fine Bavarian beer is here,
As good as you have tasted.
It runs through all the streams in town,
And not a drop is wasted. *Chorus*

Aa Laxene dem springer
Saa lysting in Bække,
Dem hopper selve i Gryden aa roper:
Dem ska' dække! *Chorus*

The salmon leap into the kettle
Fast as they are able.
Then they wiggle from the pot
Right onto the table. *Chorus*

Aa brunstegte Griser
De løber om saa flinke,
Aa forespør sig høfligt,
Om Nogen vil ha' Skinke. *Chorus*

Rushing 'round the streets,
Roasted piggies cause a traffic jam,
Inquiring so politely if
Perchance you'd like a slice of ham. *Chorus*

Aa Kjørene dem melker
Aa kjærner aa yster
Liksaa naturlig
Som Else, mi Syster. *Chorus*

And the cows, they milk themselves.
Please believe me, mister.
Then they churn out cheese as good as
Does Else, my sister. *Chorus*

Aa Kalvene de slagter sig
Hurtig og flaar sig,
Aa stejker sig fortere
End man tar en Taar sig! *Chorus*

And the calves, they kill themselves
Right before your very eyes.
Then roast veal is served to all,
Quicker than you realize. *Chorus*

Aa Høna værper Æg
Saa svære som Stabur,
Mens Hanen angir Tiden
Som et ottedags Slaguhr. *Chorus*

The hens lay eggs so big,
Their size surely would give you a shock.
And the roosters strike the hour
As well as an eight-day clock. *Chorus*

Aa Maanen hver Aften er fuld
Det er sikkert.
Jeg ligger just aa ser paa'n
Med Flaska tel Kjikkert. *Chorus*

There is a full moon every night,
So there is no need to grope.
I am observing it right now—
My bottle for a telescope. *Chorus*

Ja to Daler Dagen
Det faar Du for at svire,
Aa er Du rektig doven,
Saa kanske Du faar fire. *Chorus*

When you go carousing,
You'll get two dollars, and what's more,
If you do it very well,
They will surely give you four. *Chorus*

15

Fra Skyerne det regner
Med Kolerakaker.
As Gubervare Dere vel
For dejlige Saker!   *Chorus*

Kronarbejde findes ej-
Nej det var saa ligt da!
Jeg sad nok ikke ellersen
Saa frisk her aa digta.   *Chorus*

Vi gaar i Fløjelsklæder
Besat med Sølverknapper,
Aa ryker af Merskum,
Som Kjærringa stapper.   *Chorus*

Aa Kjærringa maa brase
Aa styre aa stelle–
Aa blir hu sint, saa banker hu sig selv-
Skal jeg fortælle.   *Chorus*

As Fiolin det speller
Vi allesammen — hejsan!
Aa Danser en Polskdans.
As den er'nte lejsan.   *Chorus*

Ja rejs til Oleana,
Saa skal Du vel leve,
Den fattigste Stymper
Herover er Greve!   *Chorus*

Cakes and cookies rain down
From the heavens day and night.
Good Lord, they are so delicious,
They're a source of great delight.   *Chorus*

No need to support your kids,
And to fill their purses.
If I had to work I couldn't
Sit here spinning verses.   *Chorus*

Velvet suits with silver buttons,
We all wear without a fuss.
And we smoke our meerschaum pipes,
Which the old woman fills for us.   *Chorus*

And she has to sweat and toil,
All her work completing.
If she doesn't finish it,
She gives herself a beating.   *Chorus*

Everyone plays violin,
And dances polkas daily.
Life is very pleasant here,
We pass the time so gaily.   *Chorus*

So just you go to Oleana,
And you'll never have a care.
The poorest wretch in Norway
Becomes a count once over there.   *Chorus*

Repeat first verse

16

Il Grillo E La Formica
The Grasshopper And The Ant

Italy (Piedmont)

Lu gril a canta Sü la ra—ma del lin, Lu gril a can—ta Sü
Grass—hop—per sing — ing All un—der a lime tree, Grass—hop—per sing — ing All

la ra—ma del lin, S'ai pas—sa la für—mia Na' di—man—da un tan—tin.
un—der a lime tree, An ant came by and asked,"Have you a coin for me?"

Lu gril ai ciama
Cosa t'na veule fè?)2
Veuj fe braje e camise
E mi veuj maridè.

Lu gril ai ciama
Vureisse pieme mi?)2
Fürmia l'è staita lesta
Oh s'a l'a djie che'd si.

Lu gril a saöta
Per buteje l'anel)2
S'antrapa nt'una pera
E s'romp'l so servel.

E la fürmia
L'è andaita a Pineröl)2
Cômprese 'na vestiña
Per pôdej fe'l deul.

Grasshopper asked her
If she'd explain her plan,)2
"I want to buy a wedding ring,
And get a man."

Grasshopper asked her
If she would be his bride,)2
"Why I would simply be delighted,"
She replied.

Grasshopper jumped up,
The ring for to present,)2
He cracked his head against a pear,
And that's the way it went.

So the ant went off
To Pinerolo town,)2
And bought herself a somber
Pitch-black mourning gown.

Pust Vsegda Budet Solntse
Let The Sun Shine Forever

USSR
Russian Words by Lev Oshanin
Music by A. Ostrovskii

Milyi moi drug, vernyi moi drug,
Liudiam tak khochetsia mira!
I v tridtsat' piat' serdtse opiat'
Ne ustayot povtoriat': *Chorus*

Tishe, soldat, slyshish' soldat,
Liudi pugaiutsia vzryvov.
Tysiachi glaz v nebo gliadiat,
Gubi upriamo tverdiat. *Chorus*

Protiv bedy, protiv voiny
Vstanem za nashikh mal'chishek.
Solntse navek, schast'e navek, –
Tak povelel chelovek! *Chorus*

Oh, my good friend, oh, my true friend,
Mankind wants peace the world over!
Whether at five or thirty five
People repeat as they strive: *Chorus*

Soldier, be still, hear if you will,
People are scared of explosions.
Thousands of eyes look to the skies,
And people speak out and say: *Chorus*

Hunger no more, and no more war.
We stand behind our children.
Let there be sun, let there be fun –
That's what we want - everyone! *Chorus*

Shalom, Chaverim
Peace, Brothers

Israel

This is a round which may be sung in as many as eight parts. The Roman numerals indicate where the voices may enter. The Hebrew words simply mean: "Peace, brothers . . . 'til we meet again."

Hojita De Guarumal
Little Leaf Of The Guarumal

Panama

Ho - ji - ta de gua-ru - mal, Don - de vi - ve la lan - gos - ta, Don-de
Lit-tle leaf of the gua-ru - mal, That's where you can find the lo - cust, And he

co - me, don - de duer - me, Don - de vi - ve la lan - gos - ta.
eats there, and he sleeps there, That's where you can find the lo - cust

Hojita de guarumal,
Donde vive la langosta,
Donde come, donde cena,
Donde duerme la langosta.

Hojita de guarumal,
Donde vive la langosta,
Donde come, donde toma,
Donde duerme la langosta.

Hojita de guarumal,
Donde vive la langosta,
Donde come, donde duerme,
Donde muere la langosta.

Little leaf of the guaramal,
That's where you can find the locust.
And he eats there, and he sups there,
That's where you can find him sleeping.

Little leaf of the guarumal,
That's where you can find the locust.
And he eats there, and he drinks there,
That's where you can find him sleeping.

Little leaf of the guaramal,
That's where you can find the locust.
And he eats there, and he sleeps there,
That's where he will die, the locust.

Mi Caballo Blanco
My White Horse

Chile

Es mi ca-ba-llo blan-co, co-mo un a-man-e-cer,
White is my hors-es col-or, white as the morn-ing dawn,

Siem-pre jun-ti-tos va-mos; Es mi a-mi-go mas fiel.
We al-ways ride to-geth-er; He is my faith-ful friend.

Chorus

Mi ca-ba-llo, mi ca-ba-llo, gal-o-pan-do va.
My faith-ful horse, my faith-ful horse, gal-lo-ping a-long.

En alas de una dicha
Mi caballo corrió,
Y en brazos de una pena
También êl me llevó. *Chorus*

Hasta que a Dios le pido
Que lo tenga muy bien,
Si a su lado me llama,
En mi blanquito iré. *Chorus*

Riding on wings of gladness,
My white horse carried me.
And in the arms of sadness,
Together we shall be. *Chorus*

I ask the Lord to keep him,
Safe - and to be his guide.
And when the Lord shall call me,
On Whitey I shall ride. *Chorus*

El Zancudo
The Mosquito

Colombia

E – ché mis per – ros al mon – te, El u – no la – tió muy
I sent my dogs to the moun – tain, And there was a loud com –

du – ro. El a – mo se fue a – so – mar, Y er' un in – fe – liz zan –
motion. When I ran up and looked a – round, A mo – squi – to was set in

cu – do. Cla – vé mi ro – dill – a en tier – ra, Y a – pun – té bien a – pun
mo – tion. I dug my heel in the ground then, And care – ful – ly aimed my

ta – o, Y fue tan grand' el ba – la – zo Que que – dó pa – ta – rri – ba o
ri – fle, The bul – let, it hit him so hard, That you know it was no tri – fle.

Pa matar ese animal
Se tendió l'infantería
Con quince ametralladoras
Y un cañón d'infantería.
  La carne d'este animal
  La mandaron pa Marmato
  Pesaba dos mil arrobas,
  Catorce libros y cuarto.

El sebo d'este animal
Lo mandaron p'al Tabor.
Eso hace quinientos años,
Y todavía hay jabón.
  Del cuero d'ese animal
  Salieron dos mil paraguas,
  Y un pedazo que sobró
  Se lu'hizo una vieja en naguas.

In order to kill this monster,
The army, it had to be called up,
With fifteen machine guns blazing-
A cannon was also rolled up.
  The flesh of this great mosquito
  Was sent off to feed Marmato.
  Five thousand pounds it did weigh,
  Plus forty more pounds and a quarter.

The fat of this great mosquito
Was sent over to Tabor.
That was five hundred years ago-
Of soap, they still need no more.
  The hide yielded up two thousand
  Umbrellas for rainy weather.
  And from the small piece left over,
  A fine skirt was stitched together.

El Cascabel
The Little Bell

Mexico

25

Bonito tu cascabel,
Vida mía, ¿Quién te lo dio? ⎤
Vida mía, ¿Quién te lo dio? ⎦ 2
Bonito tu cascabel.
¡A mí no me lo dio nadie! (2)
Mi dinero mi costó.
Y quien quiera cascabel,
¡Que lo compre como yo! *Chorus*

Oh, your bell is very nice.
Tell me, dear, who gave it to you? ⎤
Tell me, dear, who gave it to you? ⎦ 2
Oh, your bell is very nice.
No one gave me this little bell! (2)
I paid for it with my money.
And if you want one as well,
You'll have to buy it just like me. *Chorus*

La Bamba

Mexico

Repeat these 2 measures ad lib before going to next verse

Final ending

Para bailar La Bamba,	If you would dance La Bamba,
Para bailar La Bamba	If you would dance La Bamba
Se necesita unos pies ligeritos,	You need little feet that are nimble,
Unos pies ligeritos y otra cosita. *Chorus*	Little feet that are nimble and one more thing. *Chorus*

Yo te canto La Bamba,	I will sing you La Bamba,
Yo te canto La Bamba	I will sing you La Bamba
Sin prentesion, porque pongo delante,	**Without a fuss — for I put my heart in it,**
Porque pongo delante mi corazón. *Chorus*	For I put my heart in it for both of us. *Chorus*

Las Mañanitas
Morning Greetings
(Birthday song)

Mexico

G

Es – tas son las ma – ña – ni – – tas que can – ta – – ba el rey Da –
Now we sing this morn-ing greet — ing, As king Da – vid used to

D7

G

C

vid. Hoy por ser día de tu san – to te las can –
do, For to – day is some-thing spe – cial – so hap – py

G

Em

D7

ta – mos a tí. Des – pier – ta, mi bien, des –
birth – day to you. A – wak – en, my dear, a –

G

Ddim *Chorus* **D7**

G

pier – ta, Mi – ra que ya a – ma – ne – ció, Ya los
wak – en, Just look, see the dawn is near; And the

D7

G

30

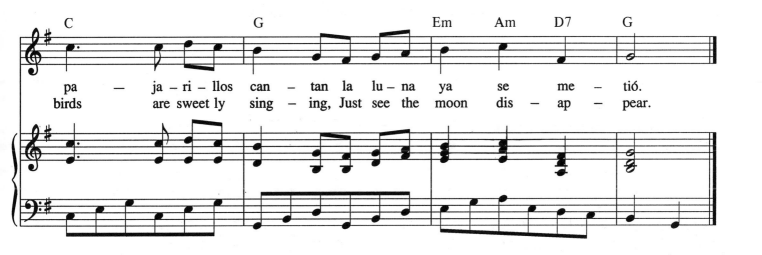

pa — ja – ri – llos can – tan la lu – na ya se me – tió.
birds are sweet ly sing – ing, Just see the moon dis – ap – pear.

Si el sereno de las esquina
Me quisiera hace favor,
De apagar su lanternita
Mientras que pasa mi amor. *Chorus*

Amapolita morada
De los llanos de Tepic,
Si no estás enamorada,
Enamórate de mí. *Chorus*

Ahora sí señor sereno,
Le agradezco su favor;
Encienda su lanternita,
Ya ha pasado mi amor. *Chorus*

Oh lamplighter on the corner,
Please just listen to my song,
And blow out your little lantern
As my love passes along. *Chrous*

Little poppy, scarlet poppy,
On the meadows growing free,
If you're not in love with someone,
Please fall in love then with me. *Chorus*

Oh lamplighter, I do thank you
For the favor that you've done.
Now you can relight your lantern,
Because my love's come and gone. *Chorus*

Echen Confites
Scatter The Candy

Mexico

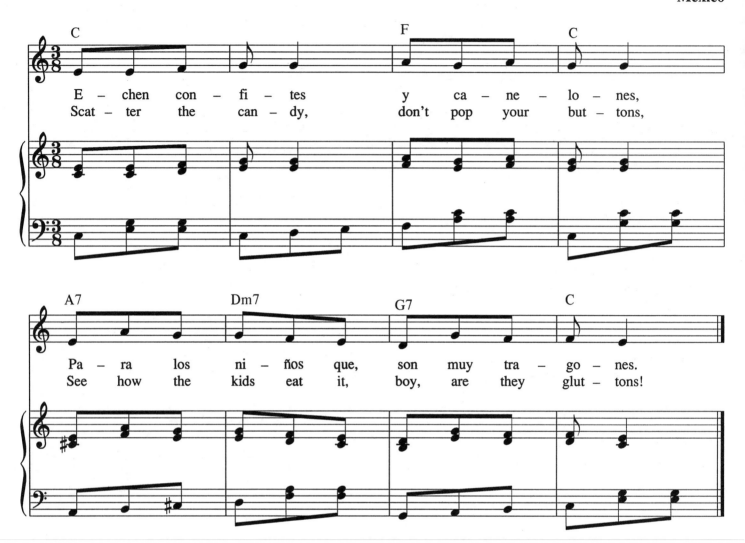

Anda nenita, no te dilates,
Con la cansata de los cacahuetes.

¡No quiero oro, ni quiero plata,
Yo lo que quiero es quebrar la piñata!

Hurry up, missy, you're driving me nuts,
Bring on that basket full of good peanuts.

I don't want gold or a silver platter,
What I want most is to break the *piñata!*

*A piñata is a hollow plaster or paper-maché container filled with Christmas presents. It is hung from the ceiling by a string and must be broken open with a stick for the presents to be revealed.

La Rana
The Frog

Mexico

1. Es – ta – ba la ra – na can – tan – do de ba – jo el
The frog, he was sing – ing a mel – o – dy un – der the

a — gua;_____ Cuan – do la ra – na se pu – so a can –
wa — ter;_____ And when the frog was a – let – ting it

tar, Vi – no la mos – ca y la hi – zo ca – llar._____ 2. Ca –
ring, Up came the fly and said, "Don't you sing!"_____ The

lla – ba la mos – ca a la ra – na, que es – ta – ba can – tan – do de – ba – jo el
fly, he did si – lence the frog, who was sing – ing a mel – o – dy un – der the

Add 1 more measure here for each
verse. Repeat as necessary

33

3. Callaba la araña a la mosca, la mosca a la rana, que
   estaba cantando debajo del agua;
   Cuando la araña se puso a cantar,
   vino el ratón y la hizo callar.

4. Callaba el ratón a la araña, la araña, a la mosca, la
   mosca a la rana que estaba cantando debajo del agua;
   Cuando el ratón se puso a cantar,
   vino el gato y lo hizo callar.

5. Callaba el gato al ratón el ratón a la araña,
   la araña a la mosca, la mosca a la rana que estaba
   cantando debajo del agua;
   Cuando el gato se puso a cantar,
   vino el perro y lo hizo callar.

6. Callaba el perro al gato, el gato al ratón, el ratón a
   la araña, la araña a la mosca, la mosca a la rana
   que estaba cantando debajo del agua;
   Cuando el perro se puso a cantar,
   vino el palo y lo hizo callar.

3. The spider did silence the fly, and the fly stopped
   the frog, who was singing a melody under the water;
   And when the spider was letting it ring,
   Up came the rat and said, "Don't you sing!"

4. The rat he did silence the spider, the spider the fly, and
   the fly stopped the frog who was singing a melody
   under the water; And when the rat was letting it ring,
   Up came the cat and said, "Don't you sing!"

5. The cat he did silence the rat, who did silence the
   spider, the spider the fly, and the fly stopped the frog
   who was singing a melody under the water;
   And when the cat was letting it ring,
   Up came the dog and said, "Don't you sing!"

6. The dog he did silence the cat, who did silence the rat,
   who did silence the spider, the spider the fly, and the
   fly stopped the frog who was singing a melody under
   the water; And when the dog was letting it ring,
   Up came the stick and said, "Don't you sing!"

7. Callaba el palo al perro, el perro
al gato, el gato al ratón, el ratón a la araña,
la araña a la mosca, la mosca a la rana que estaba
cantando debajo del agua;
Cuando el palo se puso a cantar;
vino el fuego y lo hizo callar.

8. Callaba el fuego al palo, el palo al perro, el perro
al gato, el gato al ratón, el ratón a la araña, la araña a
la mosca, la mosca a la rana que estaba cantando
debajo del agua;
Cuando el fuego se puso a cantar,
vino el agua y lo hizo callar.

9. Callaba el agua al fuego, el fuego al palo,
el palo al perro, el perro al gato, el gato al ratón,
el ratón a la araña, la araña a la mosca,
la mosca a la rana que estaba cantando
debajo del agua;
Cuando el agua se puso a cantar,
vino el toro y la hizo callar.

10. Callaba el toro al agua, el agua al fuego, el fuego al
palo, el palo al perro, el perro al gato, el gato
al ratón, el ratón a la araña, la araña a la mosca,
la mosca a la rana que estaba cantando debajo
del agua;
Cuando el toro se puso a cantar,
vino el cuchillo y lo hizo callar.

7. The stick he did silence the dog, who did silence the
cat who did silence the rat, who did silence the spider,
the spider the fly, and the fly stopped the frog who was
singing a melody under the water;
And when the stick was letting it ring,
Up came the fire and said, "Don't you sing!"

8. The fire did silence the stick, who did silence the dog,
who did silence the cat, who did silence the rat, who
did silence the spider, the spider the fly, and the fly
stopped the frog who was singing a melody under the
water; And when the fire was letting it ring,
Up came the water and said, "Don't you sing!"

9. The water did silence the fire, who did silence the
stick, who did silence the dog, who did silence the cat,
who did silence the rat, who did silence the spider, the
spider the fly, and the fly stopped the frog who was
singing a melody under the water;
And when the water was letting it ring,
Up came the bull and said, "Don't you sing!"

10. The bull did silence the water, who silenced the fire,
who did silence the stick who did silence the dog, who
did silence the cat, who did silence the rat, who did
silence the spider, the spider the fly, and the fly
stopped the frog who was singing a melody under the
water; And when the bull was letting it ring,
Up came the knife and said, "Don't you sing!"

Duérmete, Niño Lindo
Oh Sleep, My Little Baby

Mexico-New Mexico

This lullaby from the Christmas pageant "Los Pastores" was introduced by the Spanish missionaries into New Mexico during the 16th century. When the Spaniards were driven out of New Spain in 1821, many parishes were left without "padres." But "Los Pastores" and other folk dramas and songs were spread into Spanish-speaking communities throughout the Southwest. The pageant is still performed both in communities and schools.

Duér - me - te, Ni - ño lin - do, _____ en los bra - zos
Oh sleep my lit - tle Ba - by, _____ ly - ing in the

del _____ a - mor, _____ Que te a - rro - lla tu
arms _____ of love, _____ While your_ moth - er

ma - dre _____ can - tan - do te a - la - rru. _____
sings you _____ a lul - la - by from a - bove. _____

No temas a Herodes,
Que nada te ha de hacer.
En los brazos de tu madre,
Nadie te ha de ofender. *Chorus*

Oh, have no fear of Herod,
He can do no harm to you,
Here in the arms of your mother
While she sings alarru. *Chorus*

Sur Le Pont D'avignon
On The Bridge At Avignon

France

Chorus

Sur le pont____ d'A – vi – gnon. L'on y dan – se, L'on y dan – se.
On the bridge at A – vi – gnon. They are dan – cing, They are dan – cing.

Sur le pont____ d'A – vi – gnon, L'on y dan – se tout en rond.
On the bridge at A – vi – gnon, They are dan – cing in a round.

Verse

Les beaux mes–sieurs font comme ci, Et puis en–core comme ça
The hand–some men bow like this, And then they bow like that.

D.C.

Les belles dames font come ci,
Et puis encore comme ça. *Chorus*

Les militaires font comme ci,
Et puis encore comme ça. *Chorus*

Les matelots font comme ci,
Et puis encore comme ça. *Chorus*

Les jardiniers font comme ci,
Et puis encore comme ça. *Chorus*

Les charpentiers font comme ci,
Et puis encore comme ça. *Chorus*

Les cordonniers font comme ci,
Et puis encore comme ça. *Chorus*

The ladies all bow like this,
And then they bow like that. *Chorus*

The soldiers all bow like this,
And then then they bow like that. *Chorus*

The sailors all bow like this,
And then they all bow like that. *Chorus*

The gardeners bow like this,
And then they all bow like that. *Chorus*

The carpenters bow like this,
And then they bow like that. *Chorus*

The shoemakers bow like this,
And then they all bow like that. *Chorus*

La Chèvre
The Nanny Goat

France

Il é – tait u – ne chèvre de fort tem – pé – ra – ment, Qui
There was a nan – ny goat, a char – ac – ter was she, When

re – ve – nait d'Es – pagne et par – lait l'al – le – mand! Oh!
she came back from Spain, spoke Ger – man flu – ent – ly! She

Bal – lu – tant d'la queue, et gri – gno – tant des dents, Elle
Swung her tail a – round, ground her teeth noi – si – ly, Came

re – ve – nait d'Es – pagne et par – lait l'al – le – mand!
back from Spain, And she spoke Ger – man flu – ent – ly!

40

Elle revenait d'Espagne et parlait l'allemand!
Elle entra par hasard dans le champ d'un Normand!
  Oh! Ballotant d'la queue et grignotant des dents,
  Elle entra par hasard dans le champ d'un Normand.

Elle entra par hasard dans le champ d'un Normand,
Elle y vola un chou qui valait bien trois francs!
  Oh! Ballottant d'la queue et grignotant des dents,
  Elle y vola un chou qui valait bien trois francs!

Elle y vola un chou qui valait bien trois francs,
Le Normand l'assigna devant le Parlement!
  Oh! Ballottant d'la queue et grignotant des dents,
  Le Normand l'assigna devant le Parlement!

Le Normand l'assigna devant le Parlement,
La Chevre comparut et s'assit sur un banc!
  Oh! Ballotant d'la queue et grignotant des dents,
  Le chevre comparut et s'assit sur un banc!

La chevre comparut et s'assit sur un banc!
Puis elle ouvrit le Code et regarda dedans!
  Oh! Ballotant d'la queue et grignotant des dents,
  Puis elle ouvrit le Code et regarda dedans!

Puis elle ouvrit le Code et regarda dedans,
Elle vit que son affaire allait fort tristement.
  Oh! Ballotant d'la queue et grignotant des dents,
  Elle vit que son affaire allait fort tristement!

Elle vit que son affair allait fort tristement,
Lors, elle ouvrit la porte et prit la clef des champs!
  Oh! Ballotant d'la queue et grignotant des dents,
  Lors, elle ouvrit la porte et prit la clef des champs!

When she came back from Spain — spoke Germany fluently,
One day she chanced upon a farm in Normandy!
  She swung her tail around, ground her teeth noisily,
  One day she chanced upon a farm in Normandy!

One day she chanced upon a farm in Normandy,
And stole a cabbage that was worth francs one-two-three!
  She swung her tail around, ground her teeth noisily
  And stole a cabbage that was worth francs one-two-three!

She stole a cabbage that was worth francs one-two-three,
She was arrested and sent off to a jury.
  She swung her tail around, ground her teeth noisily,
  She was arrested and sent off to a jury!

She was arrested and sent off to a jury,
The goat appeared and took her seat for all to see!
  She swung her tail around, ground her teeth noisily,
  The goat appeared and took her seat for all to see!

The goat appeared and took her seat for all to see,
She read the Law and then spoke out most naturally!
  She swung her tail around, ground her teeth noisily,
  She read the Law and then spoke out most naturally!

She read the Law and then spoke out most naturally,
When she saw that the judge would show her no mercy!
  She swung her tail around, ground her teeth noisily,
  When she saw that the judge would show her no mercy!

When she saw that the judge would show her no mercy,
She opened up the door and ran to liberty!
  She swung her tail around, ground her teeth noisily,
  She opened up the door and ran to liberty!

Mon Papa
My Papa

France

Mon pa - pa ne veut pas que je dan - se, que je dan - se,
He says no, my pa - pa, No more dan - cing, no more dan - cing.

Mon pa - pa ne veut pas que je dan - se la pol - ka!
He says no, my pa - pa, No more dan - cing the pol - ka!

Mais, malgré sa defense,
Moi je danse, moi je danse,
Mais malgré sa defense,
Moi je danse la polka!

But despite my papa
I'll keep dancing, I'll keep dancing,
But despite my papa,
I'll keep dancing the polka!

Voici L'Hiver Bientôt Passé
Winter Will Soon Be Passed Away

France

Voi - ci l'hi - ver bien - tôt pas - sé, Le doux prin - temps ap - pro - che.
Win - ter will soon be passed a - way, Spring - time is get - ting clos - er.

Fine

Cet - te sai - son tant dé - si - rée par nous et par les au - tres.
You can hear all the chil - dren say, It's the best time we know, sir.

D.C. al Fine

Le Corbeau Et Le Renard
The Crow And The Fox

France-Canada

Un jour, Maî-tre Cor-beau, sur un ar-bre per-ché, Te-nait de-dans son bec un fro-mage bien â-gé. Le Ca-pi-taine Re-nard, at-ti-ré par l'o-deur, L'ac-cos-te po-li-ment par un pro-pos flat-teur. Sur l'air du

One day a crow was sit-ting 'way up in the trees, And in his beak he held a piece of rip-ened cheese. A-long came Cap-tain Fox — who'd smelled it from a-far, And said to Mas-ter Crow, "What a fine bird you are!" A sing-ing

Chorus

tra la, la, la; sur l'air du tra la, la, la. Sur
tra la, la, la; a – sing – ing tra la, la, la. A –

l'air du tra dé – ri, dé – ri, dé – ra, tra la, la.
sing – ing tra de – ri, de – ri, de – ra, tra la, la.

'Mes sincères compliments, cher Monsieur le Corbeau,
Dans ce chic habit noir, ah, que vous êtes beau!
Et si votre ramage égale vos atours,
Vous êtes le phénix des forêts d'alentour!" *Chorus*

L'corbeau, ravi d'avoir un auditeur de choix,
Ouvre son large bec pour mieux montrer sa voix.
Le bon fromage, hélas à terr' ne fit qu'un saut,
Le renard s'en saisit et l'corbeau fut très sot! *Chorus*

Car l'autre sa régale et, sur un ton moqueur,
Lui dit: "Maître Corbeau, gardez-vous des flatteurs!
Je vous joue un bon tour, et parbleu, c'est bien fait!
Bonsoir, j'avais grand' faim, et l'fromage est parfait!" *Chorus*

"My compliments to you, my dearest Mister Crow,
For in your stylish black suit, how your feathers glow;
And if your singing voice does equal your attire,
The other creatures of the woods you would inspire!" *Chorus*

The crow, he was delighted by his friend so choice.
He opened up his beak to better show his voice.
The piece of cheese, alas, it fell down to the ground.
The fox, he pounced upon it with a single bound. *Chorus*

And in a mocking tone, while gulping down the cheese,
The fox said, "Mister Crow, beware of flatteries.
You really must admit I fooled you through and through.
The cheese it was superb - and so, goodnight to you!" *Chorus*

Alouette
The Skylark

Canada

Alouette, ("the skylark") is known and sung in French by children all over the world. It means: Skylark, gentle skylark, I will pluck your feathers. I will pluck your head . . . beak . . . neck . . . legs . . . feet.

A - lou - et - te, gen - tille A - lou - et - te, A - lou - et - te,

Je te plu - me - rai. Je te plu - me - rai

1. La tête,
2. Le bec,
3. Le cou,
4. Les jambes,
5. Les pieds,

Repeat cumulatively back to "tête" as song progresses.

Et 1. La tête, Et 1. La tête,
2. Le bec, 2. Le bec,
3. Le cou, 3. Le cou,
4. Les jambes, 4. Les jambes,
5. Les pieds, 5. Les pieds,

A - lou - ette, A - lou - ette, Oh, _____

D.C. al Fine

A Fidler
A Fiddler

Jewish

S'hot der ta – te fun ya – ri dl Mir ge – bracht a na – ye fi – dl.
Once when I was ve – ry lit – tle, Pa – pa brought me home a fid – dle.

Chorus

Do re mi fa sol la si, Shpil ich di – dl – di di, di.
Do re mi fa sol la si, I play did – dle dee dee, dee.

Shpil ich di – dl – di di.
I play did – dle dee, dee.

Ch'halt dos kepl ongeboygen,
Un farglots di beyde oygn. *Chorus*

Rechtn fus faroys a bisl,
Klap dem takt tsu mitn fisl. *Chorus*

Kvelt un vundert zich di mame,
"Kenst doch azoy gut di game!" *Chorus*

Hold my head at the right angle,
Do not let the fiddle dangle. *Chorus*

With my right foot out I must stand,
Counting, tapping, "One-and, two-and." *Chorus*

Mama can't keep herself steady,
"See, he knows the scale already!" *Chorus*

Hänschen Klein
Little Hans

Germany

Häns – chen klein, ging al – lein, in die wei – te Welt hin – ein.
One fine day, so they say, lit – tle Hans he went a – way.

Stock und Hut steht im gut, ist ja wohl – ge – mut.
Staff in hand o'er the land, he was feel – ing grand.

A – ber Mut – ter wein – et sehr, hat ja nun kein Häns – chen mehr.
But his moth – er, she felt pain, want – ed her Hans home a – gain.

Da be – sinnt, sich das Kind, Eilt nach Haus ge – schwind.
He turned 'round, with a bound, Ran home safe and sound.

Lieb Mama, ich bin da,
Ruft das Hänschen, hopsasa.
Bleib bei dir, glaub es mir,
Geh nicht mehr von hier.
Da freut sich die Mama sehr,
Und das Hänschen noch viel mehr,
Dann es ist, wie ihr wisst,
Schöner doch bei ihr.

Mama dear, I am here,
Hans called out both loud and clear.
This I say, I will stay,
And won't go away.
Mama, she felt very glad,
Hans was feeling far from sad.
Home was best, Hans confessed,
Better than the rest.

Gestern Abend Ging Ich Aus
In the Evening Yesterday

Germany

Ges – tern Ab – end ging ich aus, ging wohl in den Wald hin – aus.
In the eve – ning yes – ter – day, to the woods I made my way.

Sass en Häs – lein in dem Strauch, guckt mit sein – em Aug – lein raus.
There a rab – bit I did spy, peep – ing out, he winked his eye.

Kommt das Häs – lein dicht her – an, das mir's was er – zäh – len kann.
Then as quick as one, two, three, He came up and spoke to me.

Bist du nicht der Jägersmann,
Hetzt auf mich die Hunde an.
Wenn dein Winspiel mich erschnappt,
Hast du, Jäger, mich ertappt.
Wenn ich an mein Schicksal denk,
Macht es mich von Herzen krank.

Armes Häslein, bist so blass,
Geh dem Bau'r nicht mehr in's Gras.
Geh dem Bau'r nicht mehr in's Kraut,
Sonst bezählst's mit deiner Haut.
Sparst dir manche Not un Pein,
Kannst mit lust ein Häslein sein!

You're the hunter, that I see,
And you set your dogs on me.
When your greyhound tries to bite,
And to catch me — what a fright!
When upon my fate I think,
The my heart begins to sink.

Little rabbit, understand,
Don't go on the farmer's land.
And his cabbage leave aside,
Or you will pay with your hide.
Spare yourself much grief and woe,
And then I will let you go.

Es Klappert Die Mühle
The Mill Is A-Clanking

Germany

Es Klap-pert die Müh-le am rausch-en-den Bach: Klipp, Klapp. Bei
The mill is a clank-ing a - long-side the stream: Clip, clop. The

Tag und bei Nacht ist der Mül-ler stets wach: Klipp, Klapp. Er
mil-ler works hard and has no time to dream: Clip, clop. He

macht uns das Korn zu den kräft-ig-en Brot, Und hab-en wir sol-ches so
chang-es the grain in-to won-der-ful bread, And there is e - nough, so we

hat's kein-e Not: Klipp, Klapp, Klipp, Klapp, Klipp, Klapp.
all can be fed: Clip, Clop, clip, clop, clip, clop.

Flink laufen die Räder und drehen den Stein:
  Klipp, klapp.
Und mahlen den Weizen zu Mahl us so fein:
  Klipp, klapp.
Der Bäcker dann Zwieback und Kuchen draus bäckt,
Der immer den Kindern besonders gut schmekt:
  Klipp, klapp., klipp, klapp, klipp klapp.

Wenn reichliche Körner das Ackerfeld trägt:
  Klipp, klapp.
Die Mühle dann flink ihre Räder bewegt:
  Klipp, klapp.
Und schenkt uns der Himmel nur immerdar Brot,
So sind wir geborgen und leiden nicht Not:
  Klipp, klapp, klipp, klapp, klipp, klapp.

The wheels turn so quickly, the stones grind away:
  Clip, clop.
They grind up the wheat into flour each day:
  Clip, clop.
The baker all sorts of delicious things **bakes,**
For children like biscuits and cookies and cakes
  Clip, clop, clip, clop, clip, clop.

When harvests of plenty are brought in the fall:
  Clip, clop.
It's then that the mill wheels turn fastest of
  Clip, clop.
For heaven does always provide us with bread,
And we are protected from sorrow and dread:
  Clip, clop, clip, clop, clip, clop.

Ein Männlein Steht Im Walde
A Little Man Stands 'Midst The Trees

Germany

Ein Männ-lein steht im Wal-de ganz still und stumm. Es hat von laut-er pur – pur ein
A lit – tle man stands qui-et-ly 'Midst the trees. He wears a pur-ple coat hang-ing

Mänt – lein um. Sag wer mag das Mann-lein sein, das da steht im Wald al-lein,
to his knees. Who's that lit – tle man un-known, stand-ing in the woods a-lone,

Mit dem pur-pur-rot – en __ Män – te – lein. Sag wer mag das Männ-lein sein,
Wear-ing his long coat of a pur – ple tone? Who's that lit – tle man un-known,

das da steht im Wald al – lein, Mit-dem pur-pur-rot – en __ Män – te – lein.
stand-ing in the woods a – lone, Wear-ing his long coat __ of a pur – ple tone.

Das Männlein steht im Walde auf einem Bein.
Es hat auf seinem Haupte schwarz Käpplein klein.
Sag wer mag das Männlein sein,
Das da steht im Wald allein,
Mit dem kleinen schwarzen Käppelein.   ] 2

The little man stands in the woods on one foot.
Upon his head a little black cap stays put.
Who's that little man unknown,
Standing in the woods alone,
Wearing his black little cap on his dome?   ] 2

The Keeper

England

The keep-er would a – hunt-ing go, And un-der his coat he
car-ried a bow, All for to shoot at the mer-ry lit-tle doe, A-
mong the leaves so green, o. *Chorus* Jack-ie boy! Mas-ter! Sing ye well? Ve-ry well!
Hey down! Ho down! Der-ry, der-ry down, A- mong the leaves so

green, o. To my hey down, down! To my ho down, down! Hey down! Ho down!

Der-ry, der-ry down. A - mong the leaves so green, o.

The first doe he shot at he missed;
The second doe he trimmed he kissed;
The third doe went where nobody wist,
Among the leaves so green, O. *Chorus*

The fourth doe she did cross the plain;
The keeper fetched her back again;
Where she is now she may remain,
Among the leaves so green, O. *Chorus*

The fifth doe she did cross the brook;
The keeper fetched her back with his crook;
Where she is now you must go and look
Among the leaves so green, O. *Chorus*

The sixth doe she ran over the plain;
But he with his hounds did turn her again;
And it's there he did hunt in a merry, merry vein.
Among the leaves so green, O. *Chorus*

The Jolly Miller

England

There was a jol – ly mill – er once lived on ___ the riv – er Dee, _____ He
worked and sang from morn till night, No lark ___ more blithe than he. _____ And _
this the bur – den of his song for – ev – er used to be, _____ I
care for no – bo – dy, no not I, And no – bo – dy cares for me. _____

I live by my mill, she is to me
Like parent, child and wife.
I would not change my station here
For any other in life.
The song shall pass in jovial round,
And go from me to thee:
I care for nobody, no not I,
And nobody cares for me.

Billy Barlow

England

"Let's go hunt – ing," says Risk – y Rob.

"Let's go hunt – ing," says Rob – in to Bob.

"Let's go hunt – ing," says Dan – 'l to Joe.

"Let's go hunt – ing," says Bil – ly Bar – low.

"What shall I hunt?" says Risky Rob.
"What shall I hunt?" says Robin to Bob.
"What shall I hunt?" says Dan'l to Joe.
"Hunt for a rat," says Billy Barlow.

"How shall I get him?" says Risky Rob.
"How shall I get him?" says Robin to Bob.
"How shall I get him?" says Dan'l to Joe.
"Borrow a gun," says Billy Barlow.

"How shall I haul him?" says Risky Rob.
"How shall I haul him?" says Robin to Bob.
"How shall I haul him?" says Dan'l to Joe.
"Borrow a wagon," says Billy Barlow.

"How shall we divide him?" says Risky Rob.
"How shall we divide him?" says Robin to Bob.
"How shall we divide him?" says Dan'l to Joe.
"Watch how I do it," says Billy Barlow.

"I'll take shoulder," says Risky Rob.
"I'll take side," says Robin to Bob.
"I'll take ham," says Dan'l to Joe.
"Tail bone mine," says Billy Barlow.

"How shall we cook him?" says Risky Rob.
"How shall we cook him?" says Robin to Bob.
"How shall we cook him?" says Dan'l to Joe.
"Each as you like it," says Billy Barlow.

"I'll broil shoulder," says Risky Rob.
"I'll fry side," says Robin to Bob.
"I'll boil ham," says Dan'l to Joe.
"Tail bone raw," says Billy Barlow.

Out Of Doors

England

Hill and val – ley or gale – swept lea, Out of doors is the life __ so free; Sum – mer light shim- mer – ing, Win – ter night glim- mer – ing, There's no path but is beck – on- ing me,

Sweet the kingdom of flowers and bees,
Soft the rustle of swaying trees.
Birds singing cheerily,
Winds piping merrily,
Where are the melodies brighter than these?

With the cattle across the moors,
Or the herring boats 'round the shores;
There is no strife in it,
Music is rife in it,
Gay the life of it, life out of doors.